Awaken the Woman Within

[redacted]

Awaken the Woman Within
7 Principles for Developing Your Authentic Self
Azizah Sulieman

ISBN 0-9790630-0-0

Published by AzizahSpeaks Publishing
P.O. Box 92938
Washington, DC 20090
www.AzizahInc.com

All scriptures quotations are taken from the King James Version of the Bible

Cover Design & Layout by Jonathan Jones
Editorial Services by Maggie Beetz

Contents

Awaken the Woman Within

7 PRINCIPLES
FOR DEVELOPING
YOUR AUTHENTIC SELF

AZIZAH SULIEMAN

Azizah Speaks
PUBLISHING
WASHINGTON, DC

Dedication

To Ada, Wanda, Caroline, JaQuata, Imani, Tracy & Georgette.

Inroduction to Awaken the Woman Within

Many women today feel a sadness we cannot name. Though we accomplish much of what we set out to do, we sense that something is missing in our lives- fruitlessly- search "out there" for the answers. What's often wrong is that we are disconnected from an authentic self."

~Emily Hancock

In today's busy world it is easy for us to get lost in work, family affairs, daily errands and endless to-do lists. We pride ourselves on our productivity and measure our success by our accomplishments. While our ability to achieve personal success is worthy a goal for which every woman should strive, many women today are experiencing a disconnect between their everyday lives and the authentic self within.

When we lose touch with ourselves we are easily led astray. We follow the objectives and value the ambitions of the people around us, instead of the person within us. Motivation is a great start, but life requires understanding, serenity and clarity to be lived completely. We must find the woman within to redirect us toward the path God intended.

The purpose of the book is to provide a guide to women who find their lives stagnated, often by reasons beyond their own understanding. As hard as we work and as busy as we are, some of us find ourselves running in circles, unable to move toward our goals. When we are tuned out to the voice of God and the voice of the woman within, we are unable to identify, let alone tackle, the obstacles that stand in our way.

Through meditation and prayer you can hear the woman who knows what's best for you. When you take the time to breathe and learn how to listen you will find that success is closer than you think. This book will guide women who choose to move forward in their lives by aligning their outer behaviors with their inner convictions and reestablishing their God-given purposes.

Learn to trust yourself and conquer your insecurities. Make plans but allow for endless revisions. Set a pace and contemplate timing. Write down your dreams. Use the resources you already possess to achieve the goals you assumed were out of reach. Finding the woman within takes discipline, patience, tolerance and acceptance. But it's still easier than you can imagine.

If you are ready to take an epic journey into your self and if you're ready to pursue the reflection, acceptance and actions needed to gain complete happiness, then close the door to the outside world, take a deep breathe and start the journey with me.

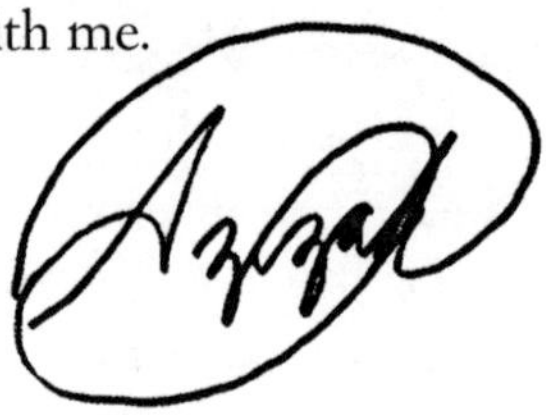

What lies behind us and what lies before us are tiny matters,
compared to what lies within us.
(Ephesians 3:20)

Principle One:
Cherish Your Visions and Your Dreams

One of the primary reasons that most women seem to live a life that lacks happiness and fulfillment is largely due to their inherent distrust of their own visions and dreams. While some of us distrust our dreams, deeming them to be of our own imaginations, some feel that their inner most beliefs and visions are too farfetched, too out of reach, capable of being achieved by someone else and not themselves. The Truth is that Visions and Dreams come from God. They are His way of putting His will for your life deep within you.

At times, God speaks to us about our future and our destiny through our dreams. Some may not know this, but consciousness and dream life are God's direct communication to man. We communicate to God through our consciences, and God in turn may communicate to us through what we call dreams. The Bible teaches us in the Old Testament that dreams may be ordinary (Job 7:14) or they may be a means through which God reveals instruction and information (Num 12:6).

The Treasure is Within You

I once read an old myth that said that long ago all people were divine. These people abused the divinity that the Father had bestowed on them so He decided to take it back and hide it somewhere they'd never find it. The only problem was that He couldn't come up with a good hiding place.

When the lesser gods were called in for council to consider the dilemma, they decided, "We will bury man's divinity deep in the earth." But the Father said, "No, that will not do, for man will dig deep down in the earth and find it." So they said, "We will sink man's divinity into the sea." But again Father replied, "No, not there either, for man will learn to dive into the deepest waters and find it."

The lesser gods then said, "We will take it to the top of the highest mountain and there we will hide it." But Father God replied, "No, for one day man will conceive how to climb even the highest mountain and take his divinity up again." The lesser gods finally gave up and concluded, "We just don't know where to hide the divinity of man, for no matter where we hide it, in the earth, or in the sea or on the mountain, there is no place that man will not eventually find it."

Then Father God said, "This is what we will do with man's divinity. We will hide it deep down within him, for he will never look there." Ever since then, the myth concludes, man has been going up and down the earth, climbing, digging, diving, exploring, searching for something that is already within himself.

And here were are today, Women of God, Women of Destiny, Women of Power, and we fruitlessly continue to look outward for something or someone to give us direction, meaning and focus in our lives. But from the foundation of the world, God put your road map to success and happiness within you.

If there is one lesson I have learned in life, it is that the nagging feeling I have in my gut to do more, be more, love more, share more, is not really a nagging at all. It is the seed of my purpose that God placed within me to grow into the daughter of destiny he has created me to be.

All the purpose you yearn for is simply God speaking to your spirit. Your wildest dreams and grandest hopes are the blessings that the Father is looking to unfold through you. It is all within your reach, for it is all within you. If it weren't so, God would not have ever placed the passion within you so deeply.

Losing focus of our dreams isn't a hard thing to do. We all have life happening to us everyday. But a key component to being your best self is doing what you were created to do. Some of us know what that is and some of us don't. We have all been graced with that inner voice, that inner vision that shows us late at night, while everyone else is sleeping, the woman that we are supposed to be.

I know for me, there were times when I couldn't sleep at night. Maybe I should say- there are times when I can't sleep at night because I know there is a woman within me who is waiting to come forth, waiting to bless the world with the gifts and talents given to her by God. There's a woman within who is waiting, she's waiting and so is God. Waiting for you too to put the blinders on to what friends, companions, family members, and collogues think you should be or who they think you are, and ready for you to say, "Yes!" to what you see in your spirit, to what you know is true in your heart.
What dreams do you have about yourself that you've haven't

shared with anyone? Is there a vision that God has revealed to you about your life and your future that you think will never come to pass? Guess what. One of the good things about God is that He never makes mistakes. If He showed it to you, it will come to pass. There is only one thing hindering your life's dream from being fulfilled and that is you. Only you can stop yourself, no one else.

I know we hear this said time and time again, but really think about it. Sit and ask yourself, why haven't I moved forward with what I know I should be doing in life? Why have I waited so long to make that one phone call that may change my life? Ask yourself, why have I sat and watched sister after sister move forward with her business, write her book, start her daycare, time and time again while I remain an observer on the sideline?

Now we can come up with many "reasons," I've learned to call them excuses, regarding why we are not following our dreams. Let's identify some ones: No money. No support. Low self esteem. Laziness. Insecurities. Friends. Environment. Idleness. Fear of Failure. Ignorance. Discipline. Time. Responsibilities. The list goes on and on. I'm sure you've thought of a lot more excuses, but ask yourself this question: Are any of these so-called "reasons" out of my control? Definitely not. You have the ability and the choice to overcome each one of these excuses and those not mentioned.

Something that became clear to me when I made the decision to move forward with my purpose is the thought that the lack of money in my life was the main cause of my stagnation. This is an untruth. What is true is that when you believe in yourself and in your dreams, God will allow others to believe in you also, hence allowing them to sow into the future of your success. I applied the principle, "do what you can with what you have," and allowed God to give the increase. When you begin applying this principle to your life, something awesome happens, the Universe responds to you and sends to you all that you need to accomplish your desired goal.

There is a great need for us to claim our entitlement within. Jesus said that the Kingdom of God is within us. When we really begin to know that we are at the center of an abundant God, we will realize that it is due to our own personal motivation, ingenuity, guidance and the unfolding of opportunities that God will let the Universe rush in and pour assistance on every side of us.

The starting point in manifesting your dreams is to accept responsibility for your own thoughts toward yourself, your money and your environment, thus taking charge of your life.

It starts with a decision, a decision to cherish what is important to you and what is best for you. It all starts and stops with you. One of the lessons I had to learn in my process is that my success and failure in life is in my control. I control if I succeed or fail- me and me alone. I thought for a long time that the reason I couldn't get my act together was because just didn't have it in me, perhaps as a result of my low self esteem. I learned something that I'd like to share with you: self esteem too is a decision. It's a decision on what you will and will not put up with in your life. Self esteem is making a decision about what is and what isn't acceptable.

My conclusion: failure is no longer acceptable in my life; neither is complacency. Living someone else's life is no longer acceptable. Conforming to individuals' thoughts regarding who I am and who I should be is not acceptable. What is acceptable is that I will only accept the best for myself; not so others can see and praise me, but because Christ is within me and as a result, I can achieve the impossible.

You too can make this decision. Decide today what is and isn't acceptable in your life. Decide that you will follow the path of your dreams, trusting that the path will lead you to a greater light. Take time now to write along the margins of this page and make your own declaration of what you will and will not accept in your life. Take the time to review your dreams and your visions. Some of us may have to brush the dust off of them, for others they are still fresh within our spirit. Whatever the case, breath life into your dreams again. Never let them die.

The late poet Langston Hughes put pen to paper and penned one of my favorite poems entitled "Dreams."

Dreams

Hold fast to dreams
For if dreams die
Life is a broken-winged bird
That cannot fly.
Hold fast to dreams
For when dreams go
Life is a barren field
Frozen with snow.

Today start journaling your dreams and describe the visions that you see. Whatever they are, no matter how crazy they would seem to others, write them down. I've come to know that there is something very powerful in journaling. Journaling allows you to track your growth; it allows you to share your most intimate thoughts and prayers that you wouldn't share with anyone, affording you the opportunity to see in writing what you want to accomplish in life.

What helped me in my transition into being a "be about it-don't talk about" person, is writing down everything thing that comes to my mind that I would want to do. Now, granted, you have to understand that everything that God gives you is not for today. God shows you some things so that you can begin preparing for the future, not for you to begin doing it now. I feel confident in saying that many individuals find a great level of frustration when they feel as though God is telling them to do many things and giving them wisdom on several projects, but nothing ever seems to come to fruition. Always remember that God's time is not our time. You may have the vision today, but He's given you the vision today so that you can begin preparing for a better tomorrow.

Taking time to journal your dreams affords you the opportunity to map out, plan, and schedule what you think you should be doing with your life. Every successful person has a personal life plan. They can tell you without hesitation what they will be doing three, five, even ten years from now. Why? Because they understand the importance of proper planning, goal setting and following the path of their dreams.

This doesn't have to be a big deal. What has helped me in the past is a five-subject spiral notepad. I have one section that stands as my master list. There, I list daily things that I need to do that will allow me to reach my goals. I break the other sections into individual chapters or projects that I am working on. For example, I have one section for a radio show. Everything in that section has all the information, contacts, telephone numbers and dates needed to assist me in reaching my goal of hosting a radio show. I have another section for a young women's empowerment club I'm working on. That section is comprised of ideas, thoughts, purposes, etc for the club and so forth.

I keep everything in this one spiral pad so that I know what I'm doing at all times. Every night before I retire, I add something on the master list from each section that is a "Must" not a "Should" that will ensure that I'm moving one step closer to achieving my goal.

It works. It may sound elementary or primary, but if you are reading this book, it's probably because you know that there is so much in you that you have to get out that seems to be hidden within and you've decided that the time is now. Try it; you have nothing to lose and a lot to gain.

The choice is yours. Live your dreams or live beneath your potential. One of the worst fates is to live a life you were never intended to live. The life you yearn for is closer than you realize. All of the happiness and success that you are seeking is already yours; it has already been given to you. It is just waiting for you to say "Yes!" by doing the footwork necessary to bring it into existence.

Many Christians are under the belief that all they have to do is pray and through a few words to God their entire life will be changed. I've applied the principle: "After you pray, move your feet!" God can do more through you than He will ever do for you. He longs to give us everything that will contribute to our highest good, but we have to do our part.

There are no dreams too great to dream, no goals too grand to achieve. We all have the inner wisdom and strength to create the life that we want by the choices that we make.

Never forget that God wants more for you than you will ever want for yourself. Awaken the Woman Within you today and allow her to shine forth. I speak a prophetic word over your life as you are reading now out of the book of Isaiah, "Arise,

Shine, for thy light has come and the glory of the Lord has risen upon thee." It's your time to shine Daughter of God. Cherish your Dreams and your Visions and allow God to manifest Himself in your life.

Never Give Up on Your Dreams

Recall with me the story of Joseph (Gen 37-41). At the age of 17 the Lord spoke to Joseph regarding the future of his life and the future of a nation. In a dream given to him by God, Joseph saw clearly who he was to become and what purpose he was to serve on the earth. In the book of Genesis, we read the story of Joseph, a dramatic portrayal of a truly good man who overcame a series of tragedies in his life and who ultimately fulfilled the plan and purposes of God.

No doubt we are assured in knowing that in his times of slavery, entrapment, imprisonment, grief and success that Joseph found comfort in a dream given to him in his youth. His dream enabled him to gain strength for his journey and the knowledge that all he was going through would not be in vain. God was within him and He would faithfully perform that which He committed to Joseph. This too should be our goal: To trust God for the things He shares with us in our lives, even when our circumstances say different. Our faith and confidence is in God and He is indeed with us.

Through the story of Joseph we learn that dreams are always conceived before they are achieved. There will always be a process between the time the dream is birthed and the time it is realized. During this time we will find our lives filled with doubts, fears, challenges and adversity. On the journey to fulfilling our dreams we will experience both good days and bad. But the question becomes, during the challenging times, do we give up or do we go on? I'd like to encourage you with an answer: Never give up on your dreams.

Not only should you never give up on your dreams, but no matter what happens, with the help of Christ, take your dreams all the way. Taking your dreams and your passions all the way can be very challenging, especially when things don't start off right. It seems for most of us, the beginning stages of our dreams always yield us more zeal than knowledge. We hit the track running with the certainty that we can conquer the world because of the belief we have inside of us. We begin this unorganized and unprepared; we say things that we shouldn't say and do things that we shouldn't do. And most of the times our journeys just don't start off the way we thought they would. But even in this time of trial and error, let us not give up on our dreams, but let us be encouraged by Joseph who through it all, continued to hold on to what seemed like an abandoned dream and continued to claim it as his own.

There will be times when your friends and family will not believe in your dream. They will not understand what you believe to be true for yourself. One of the reasons that our families are sometimes unable to have faith in our dreams is because God gave the dream to you to alone so that He can begin to build your faith and confidence in Him and His purpose for your life.

Joseph didn't receive any support from his brothers of his father concerning his dream. The Bible tells us that after he told his family of his dreams, his brothers became jealous and his father rebuked him (Gen 37:10-11). This is a reminder that it is very difficult to carry and birth your dream when your family wants you to abort it. But when God gives you your dream, your dream will carry you when you feel like you can no longer carry it.

I have learned that just because things aren't going the way I thought they should, it doesn't mean that God isn't still in control. The funny thing about dreams is that the dream is normally the ending of the story- destiny fulfilled, purposed achieved. But we never see what we have to go through to get to the end of the dream. I think that sometimes if we knew what we would have to go through to get the place of dreams fulfilled, we would turn back before we ever got started.

But Joseph never gave up:

His family members misunderstood him
He was sold into slavery
He lived in a strange land
He received favor in Potiphar's house
Potiphar's wife wrongly accused him
He was thrown into prison
He was put in charge of all the prisoners
The chief butler forgot him
He remained in prison for two years
He interpreted Pharaoh's dream
Became second in command of Egypt

Through all of this Joseph never gave up on his dreams. It was twenty-three years before he realized his dream but because he never gave up, Joseph was reconciled with his father and brothers and saved the nation of Israel. God's time is not our time. The things God may show you today may not manifest the next, but let us remember we will never know the timetable of God, but what we will know is that no matter what time of the journey we are in, we should never give up on our dreams.

Dare to Dream

Dare to dream. Dare to see yourself as someone who is capable of achieving your dreams, because you are. But remember, a dream will remain a dream until you make it a reality. Until you take the steps necessary to accomplish the thoughts, visions and ideas you have concerning your life and your future, they will remain just that- thoughts, visions and ideas.

Ralph Waldo Emerson was one of the greatest visionaries of all time. It was Emerson who said to an inspiring artist, "There is no way to success in our art but to take off your coat, grind paint, and work like a digger on the railroad, all day every day." How true this advice rings for all of us today. Everyday we must keep our nose to grind, keep our hand on the plow and work at making our dreams and desires become true for us.

The practical side of dreaming is willingness to pay the price necessary to make our dreams come true. Many of us want to become successful but many of us aren't willing to pay the price. Each day we are given endless opportunities to use our full potential to succeed. There is no such thing as luck and there are no overnight successes. It is hard work, dedication and persistence coupled with unmatched tenacity that propels individuals to success and achievement.

Allow this to be your resolve: to commit yourself to a life of consistency and determination that will produce the desires and successes you long for. Though your desire may start with a dream, it can end in a reality. And that reality can be the one that God has ordained for your life. Choose to dream, choose to achieve, and choose to soar.

Principles to Remember

I. The starting point in manifesting your dreams is to accept responsibility for your own thoughts toward yourself.

II. A Dream will remain a dream until you make it a reality.

III. Commit yourself to a life of consistency & determination that will produce the desires and successes you long for.

IV. The practical side of dreaming is willingness to pay the price necessary to make our dreams come true

Principle Two: Prepare For Your Passion

I remember when I became serious about my speaking career; I came to the conclusion that I wanted to be an Inspirational Speaker. My first priority will always be the ministry that God has entrusted me with and I would never put that into the same category as a speaking career. However, I'd made the decision that I was going to do whatever it took to pursue every opportunity to bring life and empowerment into the lives of women and girls.

I have read a plethora of books on how to become a motivational speaker. I purchased books, rented them from the library, downloaded e-books- you name it and I have it when it comes to the tools needed to start a career in the speaking business. I attended seminars to hear seasoned speakers give instruction and advice on becoming a speaker. I joined public speaking associations and online community groups; I did everything I could think of that would increase my chance of becoming a public speaker.

I also learned that when you really want something in life, the first step is to gain the knowledge needed to become effective and efficient at it. There are some people who think talent is enough. While the possession of gifts and talents are helpful in advancing in any area of life, it takes the knowledge of an art, business, career, or ministry that makes the individual guaranteed to achieve successful. Talent alone is not enough- you need to do your homework.

Whatever your choice career, business or ministry assignment, do not take for granted that you will succeed because of your ability or because of your knack for it, but rather go the extra mile to research, study and learn your profession: in doing so you will become an irreplaceable asset to yourself, your family and your community.

As I began to research my desired profession and continued speaking with prominent women and men in the industry, I continued to realize something was missing. I knew there was something I needed, some form of insight or wisdom I was to gain that I had not yet received. One of the great things I love about the Holy Spirit is that He will teach us all things. There are some revelations that we will not find in a book and there are some mysteries that the Holy Spirit Himself wants to reveal to us. Through silent prayer and meditation, it was revealed to me by the wisdom of the Holy Spirit that by Him I have within me the divine power to manifest my life and my future.

Although this fact is known by many of us, most of us never take advantage of this truth. We never really capitalize on the fact that the very same spirit that God used to move over the face of the waters in the beginning of creation is the same Spirit that lives inside of us. Just as God spoke and created the universe by His Holy Spirit, so too do we have the same ability to speak our lives and future into existence.

Upon reading book after book, realizing that there was something more to be learned, I set them aside and began to seek wisdom from the Holy Spirit. My humble prayer was "Holy Spirit, you are the Teacher of all teachers; I humbly ask that you give me the guidance needed to manifest my desire to become an inspirational speaker for women and girls. In Jesus' name, amen."

I sat in silence- something that I wasn't accustomed to doing- and waited. I waited by faith in silence believing my prayers would be answered. As I sat and meditated on the love that was flowing towards me from the Holy Spirit, He spoke to me in that still small voice and simply said, "Prepare For Your Passion."

My initial response was to question His guidance. "Prepare?" I thought, "That's what I've been doing. Reading the books, going to the seminars, asking for mentorship, this is all preparation for my passion."

Again, He whispered to me, "Prepare for Your Passion." This time, it began to make sense. It was at this time He ministered to me the principle of "Act as if." It was not something I had been taught nor had I read in any book. It was a principle taught directly to me from the Holy Spirit. He simply said to me: "Act as if you are already the person you want to become. Act as if you are already in the position you aspire to gain. Act as if you have already accomplished the goals you aspire to achieve. Act as if and allow the Universe answer to you."

It seemed strange to me. It was not something I heard preached, nor had I heard it spoken by the mentors in my life. But I knew it was the Wisdom of God speaking to me, helping to prepare me for the future, answering the desired prayers of my heart.

As you embark on your journey to Awaken the woman within, you will find that there will be laws, principles and truths laying at the foundation of your soul to be learned. They are there to serve as your and chart and guide for the life you are meant to live. Everyone has to have a set of personal laws, principles and truths that govern the way they interact with others, the way they treat themselves and determine how they are to move forward in life.

There is something powerful about declaring in the spiritual realm who you are and who you are to become. For it is in the realm of the spirit that all things are reflected in the natural. What you see in the natural has already taken place in the spiritual realm. That is why it is so important that we understand the key scripture nuggets that allow us to decree and declare a thing to be so before it is seen in the natural. To know yourself authentically, you must understand that everything you see around you is caused by the unseen spirit world. We are taught to grasp concepts in the Word of God that teach us to speak those things that are not and though they were. The book of Job also reminds us: "Thou shall decree a thing and it shall be established unto thee and the light shall shine upon thy way" (Job 22:28).

With these key scriptures close to my heart, I began to Prepare for My Passion. I began applying the "Act as if" principal taught to me by the Holy Spirit. Immediately, I began to put seminar topics and workshops together to present to churches, civic groups, as well as to corporate America. I "Acted" as though I had specific engagements already booked and set for upcoming events. I marked dates in my calendar and prepared each day as if the engagements were truly approaching. Once the dates began to get closer, I would take my clothes and put them into the cleaners. I began to believe that I really had these engagements coming near and I had to be ready. It is amazing looking back knowing that I didn't have anyone calling me, but I had believed within myself, that if I did as the Holy Spirit said, He would respond to my faith, my trust and my belief in Him.

Herein lies to key to preparing for your passion: Faith. Having faith doesn't mean sitting back and waiting for God to work a miracle for you. Remember you are the miracle. Your faith becomes the catalyst that ignites the desire within you to move forward. Within you lies the power to create and achieve great things. But you must believe and have faith in this power. And after you have generated the faith needed to achieve, then you must move your feet. I am a believer that God doesn't do the work for us but through us. We must set our goals and do the work necessary to attain them.

The truth is that we only get out of life what we put into it. Whatever your dream or your passion may be, always remember there is nothing God can do for you without your help. It is your choice to choose discipline over laziness. Bad habits are not changed by miracles, only hard work, discipline and dedication is needed to take action and to see change.

Several weeks had past and I received a call from a well-known Christian Pastor informing me that he was getting ready to embark on a national crusade. He knew it was a short notice, but asked if I could join him on his mission. I told him yes and asked what my role would be in the crusade. He told me he expected his audience to include a large number of young single mothers, looking and hoping for a change. It was his prayer that I could be a part of this life-changing assignment and could impart encouragement into the lives of the young women. In silence, I began to rejoice, and with tears of joy and butterflies in my stomach, I told him that I would be honored to be a part of such an important assignment from God. I couldn't resist telling him that the Lord had been preparing me for this event.

When we walk by faith and in the perfect will of God, there are no coincidences, no good luck, no chances and no happenstance events: only the divine manifestations of God being fulfilled. On your sacred journey to Awaken the woman within, remember that nothing just happens. All that happens to you is either God sent or God allowed.

Move Your Feet

There are some people who may write off my experience as coincidence, others may say it was a stroke of good luck; I believe that it is the ability God has given all of us to manifest our destiny by becoming obedient to the Holy Spirit and by preparing for those things that we want to see happen in our lives. The book of Joshua teaches us that God is a reactive God. Though it is not my intention to teach theology in this book, I would like to use Joshua's story to clarify my point.

We know the story of Joshua: Joshua was a minister to Moses. After Moses died, the Lord gave the charge to Joshua to lead the people of Israel. The Lord gives Joshua specific instructions in the first chapter of the book of Joshua. He tells him it is time to take his place as the new leader of Israel. And as the leader of God's chosen people, God made a promise to him that every place upon which the sole of his feet tread, God would give to him. He promises Joshua that He could never leave him or forsake him; to be strong and of good courage. He instructs Joshua that if he obeys His instructions, Joshua will make his own way prosperous and will be insured success. (Joshua 1:1-8)

This is one of my favorite passages of scriptures because it gives us insight into how God works for us. It teaches us that God will always back us up when we are in alignment with Him and His word. It makes it clear to us, that as we move our feet, as we tread upon the ground, that God is behind us blessing our steps. This doesn't teach us, as many of us have learned, that God sits high in the Heavens dictating every step of our lives as though we are puppets. But it teaches us, that as long as we live according to His word, He will follow us and bless us as we move.

I like to consider God to be more reactive than He is proactive. He is reactive in that He reacts to our faith in Him. He reacts to our obedience to His word. He reacts to our faith and belief that He will accomplish what He has promised us.

We should prepare and act as if God follows our faith, blesses our obedience and allows the manifestation of the things we are seeking to come to pass in our lives.

When I joined and participated in the crusade, I shared with the women I addressed how I prepared for my passion and manifested the opportunity to be there with them. I taught them the "Act as if principal." I shared with them the importance of allowing God to manifest your destiny by your faith in action and by moving in the direction of your dreams.

It is my custom at the end of every speaking assignment to take time to talk and share with those who are in attendance. I'm always blessed to meet woman from all across the country, who stories are not so different from my own: stories of defeat and destiny, triumph and tragedy. I love to hear their stories, so I know what to pray for and what to include in future presentations. As I stood there, each woman I spoke with, whether young or old, told me that they knew immediately that if they began preparing for their passions in ways they knew they should, they trusted that God would respond to their faith and cause their dreams to manifest.

A few months later, I began to receive emails from those same young ladies, all with testimonies on how they began manifesting their destinies by preparing for their passions. Story after story, I heard from the hearts of these young woman as they spoke with humble confidence in their ability to create the life they always knew they were chosen to live.

You too have this same ability, the creative ability to speak those things that are not as though they were. Our destiny is to become a co-creator with God, and to treasure the divinity that He has placed within us. Dr. Wayne Dyer said, "Manifesting is not about getting things that are not here. It is about attracting what is already here and is a part of you on a spiritual level." As long as you remain true to your authentic self and in right standing with God, all that you desire will be forever available to you.

Once we begin to realize that God is within us, directing us, teaching us, guiding us into the paths that he has developed for us we will begin to Awaken the woman within to a higher level and standard of living.

Always remember on your Awakening Journey that whatever you radiate you attract. That everything and everyone around you is a reflection of where you are in consciousness and in spirit. If at any moment you decide you are no longer happy with your present state, change your mind, your attitude, and change your spirit and watch your environment change. It all begins with you.

It's Never Too Late

I'd like to share with you an affirmation God gave to me at a time when I felt that I had missed destiny; He spoke to me plainly the words: "It's never too late to be the person you could have become." I believe this to be a true statement spoken to me from the love of God and by the Holy Spirit. "It's never too late" has become for me what "Live Your Best Life" is for Oprah Winfry. The more I mature and the more women I meet, I find my motto grows even more significant. "It's Never Too Late." It's never too late to prepare for your passion, it's never too late to begin again, and it's never too late to Awaken the Woman Within. You have the right and the ability to re-create yourself at anytime. God gave you this life, live it to the fullest. Your life was God's gift to you; what you do with your life is your gift to God. Make the decision today regarding the quality of woman you want to be, and be that woman. Begin making the decisions that will orchestrate your life in the direction of your chosen path. Allow the woman within you to live from the inside out. Allow her beauty, her confidence, her success, her happiness, and her femininity, light up the world. It always starts within. We try to work from the outside inward, but true beauty, happiness and spiritual peace originates from the woman within.

It's Never Too Late. Allow this aphorism to be part of your daily devotional and your mantra. Allow it to be true for you. Find comfort in the fact that wherever you are right now in life is where you should be. Make it your business not to over analyze your life with where you are, where you think you should be and why you aren't there yet. Rest in knowing that God orders your steps and you are on time.

When we move and operate in the Wisdom of God, He never allows us to miss our timing. When people compare their lives to those of others they can be left with the feeling that they missed opportunities and promises from God. There is a lesson to be learned here: our timing is not the timing of God. What He has calculated for us, only He knows. What may appear to be a delay in our sight may really be a season of preparation, processing and pruning to equip us for the lives we are meant to live, the children we are chosen to train, the husbands we are destined to marry, the businesses we are determined to operate, the books we are compelled to write and the lessons we are certain to teach.

Attempt to be at peace with your current situation. Attempt to look at it through the eyes of faith and trust in the reality that you serve a just God who has your best interest at heart. Your entire life will transform as you begin to see through the eyes of faith because you no longer allow your emotions to control how you respond to life. Instead, your reactions will be determined by your faith and trust in God.

Women can add unnecessary pressure and depression to our lives by comparing ourselves to our peers. Although not all of us will admit it, many women experience a feeling of defeat when we see other women living the kind of lifestyle that we too desire. An unhealthy way to live our lives is in the continual comparison to others. Our lives were given to us so we can accomplish our own purposes not compare our purposes to that of others. Comparisons will breed depression, which is guaranteed to rob your life of its meaning. There are times when we feel should be like someone else because that person is the same age or had the same education. But the truth is that we are all on a different journey with a different destination. It doesn't matter how far ahead someone else may appear, you can never measure your success by the life of others.

What is truth for someone else may not be truth for you. Let us learn how to appreciate our pace of advancement, maturity and growth in our awakening process. The time it takes one sister to learn a lesson may not be the same for another, hence, as one has learned and passed one of God's tests, she may be permitted to continue her path to fulfillment. Another sister may miss the lesson, fail the test and be given a re-take examine by God, allowing her to remain in the same place until the lesson is fully grasped.

It is not the will of God that any of us remain stagnant or at a level of inertia, however God does not allow us to move from one level of learning to another until the first level is both mastered and understood. Frustration and disappointment enter in when we find ourselves repeating a vicious cycle of self-perceived failure. It is this self-perception of failure that causes internal doubt, insecurity and hopelessness. As we continue to internalize what we feel to be an inability to expand past our current state or situation, we develop patterns and habits that support these beliefs. We begin internalizing thoughts such as, "I don't think I'm ever going to get out of this," or "Maybe it just wasn't meant to be for me," and "This is what I get for making those stupid mistakes, I deserve this life." All of these thoughts begin to take shape in your life by coming together not only as words spoken but by real life experiences. Your words form your world. Whether the words are spoken internally or for all to hear, the truth is that we create our lives daily by the words we speak and the thoughts we think.

We will all agree that habits are hard to break. It is even harder to break a habit that grew out of low self-esteem and self-doubt. As we continue to feed these ugly self-sabotaging habits they continue to grow until they not only become a part of us, but begin to define our very being. This vicious cycle of self-sabotage and self-hurt has must be broken and can only be broken by accepting who you really are. The first step in breaking any bad habit is admitting that the habit exists. Once we become truthful with ourselves that we are uncomfortable with our current positions we release the spirit within to begin to heal us, allowing us to become free of the past and both internal and external pressures.

Have you decided what is true for you? Have you decided what path of life you will follow? Have you taken your gifts and talents before God and asked for His wisdom in directing your steps? If you haven't, it's okay- because it's never too late. I've learned it doesn't matter is you are 16 or 66, as long as you give God a complete yes to His will for your life and determine in your mind and spirit that you are going to maximize all of the potential that was placed in you by God, that nothing or no one can stop you.

Would you like to go back to college and finish your degree? Or how about take the last few classes to become a certified fitness instructor? Have you completed the book of poems you began writing last year? If your answer is yes, I congratulate you and ask that you encourage everyone around you to prepare for their passion by moving toward their goals. If you answered no, there is still time. As long as you have the ability to pursue and the will to succeed, it's never too late.

I thought it was too late. I once thought the ministry God had given me was over. I once thought that the door had opened and because I missed the opportunity to pass through, it would never open again. I once felt that because my personal finances were in an abyss that I would never again be able to have the things I desired for my daughter and for myself. I know what it feels like to believe that everyone who once believed in you has given up on you. I can relate to the sister who feels as though she is now fighting for her life and she's fighting a fight that she knows she cannot win. I know- I've been there. Just as I can attest to feelings of hopelessness, underachievement, abandonment and failure, I can also attest that with God, you can begin again.

I had to make the decision to continue to pursue my passion. Without finances and friends, but armed with faith and favor, I made the decision that God would get the glory out of my life. I knew God had to be true and if He told me in my youth that I would accomplish great feats for Him, I believed I would do just that. I had to believe that God chose me. I had to believe that He would fulfill His will concerning my life. My situation didn't look like it, my bank account didn't reflect it and my eyes couldn't always see it, but I had to believe that God was true. I had to believe that even though I couldn't buy a candy bar on a credit card as a result of my credit history, even though I became unexpectedly pregnant, and even though I had turned my back on God, I knew that because I repented my sins, recommitted my life and again walked righteously before Him, I knew that He would honor the promise He spoke.

This is why we sometimes falter- we forget the words the Lord promised us. It's easier to remember the promise of prosperity when finances are flowing. It's easier to remember that we are prophets when people call for us to minister. But it is in the dark season, the season when no one is calling that we must remember the promises the most. During my dark season I learned one of the most important characteristics required for my awakening process- Belief.

Belief, as Webster defines it, is trust or confidence, a firmly held conviction. As you journey to Awaken the Woman Within, you have to have a strong conviction of who you know yourself to be. And if you struggle with the knowledge of who you are, have a strong trust and confidence in God that because you are His Daughter that you are someone of great worth and value. Believe that although you have changed, God does not change. Accept it as true that the promises of God will always remain in effect in and over your life.

God is a covenant keeper. We are the one who are covenant breakers. God will never renege on the covenant He made with you. The words that He allowed to be spoken over your life will never fall to the ground. Though they will never fall to the ground, should they not come to pass, it will never be because God went back on His word, but because we neglected to keep our part of the promise.

I have learned that while the promise never changes, the result of what we initially expected may change. Allow me to explain: during my early days of ministry, I knew that I was meant to launch a self-empowerment program for high school girls. I was fated to create a community program to bring young women together to form a bond of sisterhood and become positive examples in their community. I neglected to complete this assignment. Now, this turn around, although I missed that opportunity and although I know that door has not been closed in the spirit realm, I also know that God is directing me effect women and girls through another avenue. At anytime, I can gather the resources needed to develop an high school empowerment group, but because I didn't do it at that specific time, God is saying, I know you maintain the same passion to help women and girls in need, but I have another path by which I want you to reach them.

My passion remains the same, the effect remains the same, but the way by which to accomplish the mission has changed. My point is this: just because you were unable to accomplish everything you thought you should in your youth- it's never too late. God will still allow you to fulfill your passion; it just may not be the way you initially thought it would be. And that is okay, as long as you are moving toward destiny, helping others along the way and living the life you know you were created to live. God will always get the glory and you will always be at peace, not only with God but also with yourself.

Do no allow another day to go by without working toward the life you want to live. One lesson I had to remember and of which I want to admonish you is to be generous with your gifts. When we feel that no one will benefit from our talents, when we feel as though no one will be affected and that no one will have anything to gain from our gifts, we are showing God how selfish we really are. The gifts and talents given to you were not only given to you for yourself, but for your family, your community, your church and for your country.

We sometimes feel that no one is going to miss us or life will go on without benefiting from our gifts and this is partly true. Life will go on without us, but the individual life of the person you were called to help may have been a little easier if you were in place to pursue your passion. I know that your talents aren't meant to lie dormant inside of you. As long as you sit on your gift, as long as you allow others operate in the areas you know God assigned to you, you and your family will remain in stagnation, simply because you decided it was too late and that you really didn't matter.

I want to share something with you- you really do matter. Everything about you matters: you life, your personality, your persona, your smile, your beauty, your laugh- it all matters! We were not placed on earth to live a life just for ourselves; we are all here on assignment to assist in making sure that the will and glory of God is fulfilled on earth. As long as we remain selfish and insecure, we will never do our part to ensure we fulfill our destiny.

It starts now. It starts today. Before you move forward and begin reading the next chapter, I want you to set this book down, grab your notepad and a pen and write down your passions. Make a list of all of your goals and write down the steps necessary to accomplish those goals. Write down who will be impacted by your decision to begin again. Starting with yourself, your children or future children, your finances, family, community, etc, write down everyone and everything that will benefit from you and what you have to offer. Always remember, where there is a need there should be a supply and if you have the supply to fulfill the need, you will always be needed.

With this list, review it and determine the "lowest hanging fruit." What is the one item on this list that is the closest to you that you can begin working on right now? Whatever that goal or item is, begin to incorporate is into your daily routine to ensure you are working towards your passion. Remember, all God expects from us is our best. We give him our best and He will do the rest. Believe that it's never too late, because it isn't and with everything within you, begin preparing for your passion and watch as the Woman Within begins to shine through.

Principle Three: Align Your Outer Behaviors with Your Inner Convictions

It is impossible to consistently perform in a way that is inconsistent with the way you see yourself. No matter how hard you try to live your life by the standards of others, you will never know happiness and peace until you are living what is true and what is truth for you. It is when you begin to stay in touch with your inner convictions and values and begin living a life that is consistent with those convictions that you find peace of mind and success in life.

The ancient Greek aphorism, "Know thyself," and more recently Shakespeare's advice as written in Hamlet, "To thine own self be true," emphasize the universal and timeless importance of appropriate self reflection. Oprah Winfrey said, "It takes courage to be yourself." How true she is. It does take courage to be you. Absolute courage. Not only does it take courage, but it also takes faith, determination and resiliency. Faith is needed to believe that because you are alive, because you are a child of God, you not only have a right to be here but also a right to be yourself. Determination and resiliency have to be cultivated from within to have the strength not to acquiesce to your surroundings or to a culture that teaches us that beauty starts first from without.

It takes great love and courage to excavate your authentic self. We are all on a journey, a journey to find ourselves. The 20th century poet Rainer Maria Rilke said, "There is only one journey. Going inside yourself." This journey affords us the opportunity to hear from and know the woman within- our authentic self. Here, she speaks to us and teaches us what is

Truth. Here we begin to understand why we are the way we are. It is during our journey to Awaken the woman within that we begin to understand what really brings us happiness, pleasure, joy, discomfort, discontent, and satisfaction.

The Power to Become

By nature I am a very outgoing person. My personality could be considered extroverted, the one who loves to be the life of the party. I have never been afraid to speak in public. In fact, I was always the student that my peers would push to ask the teacher questions before a test so that the test would be postponed. I can remember once in grade school asking so many questions before a Science test that it prolonged the test for the follow day. The next day the teacher asked if anyone had any questions other than Azizah!

Throughout my grade school and college years, I remained the front row student who asked all of the questions and wanted all of the attention. Some said I had the "gift of gab" while others said I "talked too much." While both were probably right, I began to notice a shift in my personality as I became older. While I still loved to make everyone laugh and be the light of the room, I began to feel that there was a very private part of me that wanted to be silent.

I began reading more spiritual books, journaling and meditating. My spiritual life became most important as I found myself desiring to know and study the teachings of God. During this time my passion for prayer was birthed. While my persona remained the same, my spirit began to change. I felt my spirit maturing, my extroverted nature taking a back row seat, my need for attention shifting to a desire for solitude. I found myself unsure of who I was and who I was becoming. What I knew for sure was that a change was taking place on the inside of me.

It takes power to become the woman you know you are fated to be. Power is needed because in a world where ordinary is accepted and extraordinary is looked down upon, it is the power from within that allows us to sail a steady ship amongst the storms of our circumstances, environments and peers. It is easy to give in, but it takes true power to dare to be different.

One way to affirm this power is to listen inwardly to the voice of truth that tells us who we are, what it means to be a woman and what it means to be our authentic selves. As we listen to the power and truth within, we gain immeasurable lessons about our self-esteem, our self-value and our self-worth.

Has this ever happened to you? You realize one day the little girl you have always been is no longer the woman you have become? In a very real sense, she remains a part of you, but she no longer makes up the totality of who you are now. So now you begin to live the life outwardly of the woman you know yourself to be inwardly, however you are met by those closest to you with resistance? I feel confident answering this question with a "Yes!" for you. And if it hasn't happened, just continue on your journey, you too will have this experience.

Sometimes those closest people to us can be our big hindrances of growth. It isn't that they do not want to see us grow, they do, but they'd prefer to keep us they way they know us, the "us" they are comfortable with. To them, at times, to see us change means they too will have to change. They think that we will no longer accept them if we continue to grow while they themselves remain stagnant. So they give us a hard time about becoming more mature, confident, articulate women. Not because they are jealous and want only to see our demise, but because they are afraid of this new you, someone they've never met before. After all, no one really likes to live with strangers.

So what do you do? What do you do when you know that you are no longer the person everyone expects? The unfortunate part about becoming your authentic self is that once you begin living your authentic life, there will be some who may accuse you of being "fake" and charge you with going through some sort of identity crises. I like to think of this time as a metamorphosis rather than identity crises. Looking back, I think this has to be one of my favorite parts of my journey: the part when some people would say, "Oh, she's trying to be someone else," or "She's trying to be like someone she's not." The truth is that they were right. I was trying to be someone that I was not at the time- my authentic self.

It took me a while to become comfortable with the woman within. There I was, this young, clamorous, insecure girl who was becoming a mature, graceful and confident woman. I noticed that some people were no longer comfortable around me. They would say things like, "You think you're better than us," or ask the question, "Who do you think you are?" Not being comfortable with being an outcast, I found myself relinquishing my right to be my true self and reverted to what was common and comfortable for those closes to me.

I remember reading a quote by Nelson Mandela: "Never shrink yourself so that others will feel comfortable around you." Those words echoed so loud within my spirit. I asked God that day for the strength not to shrink and for the power to become the woman He created me to be.

When we ask, God is always there to give the answer. God wants more for us than we will ever want for ourselves. He is always there; waiting for us to come to Him with our struggles and issues so that He can give us the Wisdom we need to advance. The Bible teaches us in Proverbs Chapter 3 that Wisdom and discretion will be life to our inner selves and gracious ornaments to our outer selves. It is with this wisdom given to us by God the Bible promises, that we will walk in our way securely and in confidence.

Stop Apologizing For Who You Are

It was during this same season in my journey that I asked the Holy Spirit for guidance. I remember Him speaking to me ever so gently, as He always does. I was at a gas station in Upper Marlboro, Maryland, looking up at the beautiful summer sky, when I heard His voice speak to me, "Stop apologizing for who you are." I had no idea what He meant. I took those words to heart and began to seek Him for clarity and understanding of their meaning. "Stop apologizing for who you are." Those words became a mantra for me during my times of mediation. I began to see how I was apologizing for who I was becoming. Every time I reverted back to my old self and behaviors, I was apologizing. Each time I became the comedian in the group to ensure no one felt as though I was trying to be "better" than them, I was apologizing. Each time I downplayed an open door God had given me to speak on His behalf, I was again apologizing.

We all do it. Some unbeknownst to us, while others are aware of what is happening. But we all apologize in some way or another for who we are. It is such a sad thing that our culture does not celebrate authenticity, uniqueness and individuality. This is one reason I have found it to be most important to surround yourself with individuals who are able to celebrate your successes and become strength to you in your failures. It is imperative to only allow those people in your life who can appreciate you for who you are and who you are to become. I've learned to develop a circle of friends that I can count on to have my support in times of victory and distress and that understand God takes us all through different processes to becoming our authentic selves. Your process my not be like your friends' process, but because of the support you give to each other, you know there will never be a need to apologize for

who you are and who you are becoming.
With a repentant and thankful heart, I cried to God asking if He would walk with me through this journey of transformation. I asked that He would give me the strength needed to undertake any challenge or criticism I would receive. My prayer was "God, if you help me I will continue to move forward in your power and in your love." Because of His faithfulness, He not only gave me the strength needed to endure, but He's given me the wisdom necessary to help my sisters along the way.

It's okay to be you, whoever that may be. If you think it's hard trying to be yourself, try being someone you're not. There will always be a battle within you to be yourself. There will always be a little voice inside that tells you to be safe and be like everyone else. This little person will always tell you to blend in with the crowd and that no one likes people who are different.

But in front of this little person, is a bigger woman: a woman of courage, valor and strength that will hit you in the guts every time you dishonor yourself by trying to fit in. She speaks softly in your ear, "This is not who you are; why are you dishonoring yourself?" each time she finds you not living your Truth.

She is there to be your guide, your light and your friend. She is there to give you comfort when you feel alone and hope when you feel hopeless. She is the woman within, placed there by God to give confirmation to your authenticity. She gives you the discernment needed to make major decisions and to give the assurance that everything will work out fine.

I'm Better Today than I Was Yesterday

"Be still and know that I am God." Psalm 46:10

This is one of many mantras in my life. It is in the stillness of knowing God that we come to know our true selves. I believe that you will never come to know yourself until you know God, for it is God who gives us the lamps for our feet to light our paths.

Our paths, though very different but seemingly very similar, will lead us to a place where we begin to find peace within to know, love and accept ourselves. It is during this time that the woman that we are on the outside becomes a reflection of the woman that we are on the inside.

You will feel true confidence when your outer behavior is aligned by your inner convictions. You give meaning to your life by living only by the principles and values you believe are proper. Measure your achievements not by the standards of others but by the standards you have created for yourself. The mark of one's achievement isn't measured by advancing others but by becoming better than oneself. Everyday my goal is to be better than I was yesterday. Allow this to become your mantra: "I will be better today than I was yesterday."

Emile Coue left us with a daily mantra that has changed the lives of millions. He left us an "autosuggestion" that would change the way we see our lives and the way we see the world: Day by day, in every way, I am getting better and better! Not only should we allow these words to become part of our daily mantras, but allow them to be part of your belief system. The idea is to continue to strive and stretch to be your best self.
In every area of your life, strive to become a better person.

Write your own standards for living and commit to living them. These standards should be principles that guide your life and decisions. Write standards that are true for you which will let you live a life of authenticity and respect. Recognize the life you want to live and live that life. Identify the person you want to be and be that person. Be relentless in your pursuit to stay faithful to your path and purpose in life.

We all get off course sometimes. It's a part of the journey; but just because get we off course doesn't mean we have to stay off course. God allows for "You turns." You can turn your life around at any time and change the path you must take. I love the scripture in Proverbs that teaches us that a just man will fall seven times and get back up again (24:16).
It isn't the falling down that hurts a man, but the staying down that hinders the purpose and will of God for our lives.

Always remember that with struggles comes strength and that there is no strength without a struggle. I once read a story of a little girl who was watching a moth as it tried to struggle free from its cocoon. Her heart felt sorry for the little creature, so she looked around on the ground for a little stick. Very carefully and gently, she cut away the cocoon and freed the moth. She stood there and watched the moth try again and again to flap its wings and unsuccessfully try to fly away. At last, its wings flopped for the last time and the moth died. Sadly, the little girl sat and cried. Her older sister who stood near by and watched the event take place gave her little sister a lesson she'd never forget, "Baby Sis," she said, "it was the struggle that gave strength to the moth's wings. When you cut away the cocoon, you also cut away the experience the moth needed to gain the strength to fly." So too is our life. When we try to take the short cut, the short way out, we are only hurting ourselves. It is in the heat of the journey that we gain the strength needed to take on the storms in our lives.

None of us enjoy struggles, but we all know that they are a part of life. They are a part of life that sometimes teach us the greatest lessons and help us develop the greatest character. There is no strength without the struggle

Who or how you used to be has nothing with who you are today. You will never be able to move forward by looking back at your past. Allow your past to be just what it is- a collection of memories, and your future to be what it is-the unknown, and embrace the present for the gift that it is. All you have is now. Embrace each moment you have now by honoring yourself with aligning your outer life by you inner convictions, truths and beliefs.

It's your life; no one else will ever live it for you. Be true to yourself and watch the world become true to you.

Why Alignment?

Aligning our outer behaviors with our inner convictions sends a message to those around us that we are worthy of respect. No one respects a woman who lives her life as though she is a hypocrite. Although the intentions of her heart are honest, shame and reproach are always brought upon the woman who speaks of a life of righteousness and lives a life of riotousness. Human nature forces us to believe what we see over what we hear. I can think I hear a bear, but if what I see is a lion, I am forced to believe what I heard was a lion. The same is true with character building, we can sound as if we have ourselves together, and we can make people think by our conversations that we have accomplished great things, but people will always believe how they see you over what you claim to be.

So why alignment? The alignment of behaviors and convictions is the only way to guarantee that you become a woman of integrity, honesty, character and consistency. Alignment forces us to create standards, truths, principles and laws that dictate to us and to others our way of living. With alignment, we adjust our decisions so they are in line with the way we see ourselves and on par with our standards for living. When our outer and inner selves are in alignment we cannot claim that we are women of chastity and turn around and let our actions dissent.

Once we make the decision to dishonor the standards we have set for ourselves, we cause the woman within to shrink. She begins to feel a sense of disrespect for who she is and who she knows she is to become. Once seeds of dishonor and disrespect are cultivated, they begin to show outwardly in our actions and behaviors. This is when hypocrisy sets in and the things we say are the opposite of the things we do.

We begin to disrespect our authentic selves when, for example, as single women we know God has called us to become a vessel of honor and yet we allow ourselves to be handled by men who are not our husbands. This kind of self- dishonor forces the woman within to revert in a place of quiet retreat until we become aligned again with what we know to be truth for our lives.

It takes self-love and self-respect to align our outer behaviors with our inner convictions. You must first love and respect yourself in order to know who you are and to what you will and will not resign yourself. I've always known that I was chosen by God to be set apart for His work and His use. I always knew that my life was to be one of consecration and dedication to the Lord. But in my early years I lacked self-love and self-respect, and as a result I continued to find myself in relationships with men who didn't see me as a women worthy of respect but worthy of whatever they thought I deserved.

When we allow ourselves to become engaged in unhealthy relationships, we receive less than the promises and provisions of God. When we let ourselves succumb to the treatment of individuals who do not celebrate us, but rather tolerate us, we cause the woman within to minimize her beauty, power and splendor. Until we realize that it is our own respect and self love that matters most, no one will show us the affection we desire and deserve.

Alignment starts when you are at peace with your past, your present and your future.

To move forward and to know the kind of encounters and circumstances you will and will not accept in your life, you must first be at peace with your past. Some of us allow our past to dictate our future. Because we have a fear of repeating the same mistakes, or a fear of not being able to move or grow beyond our last set back, we are afraid to make any adjustments to our belief system for fear that whatever decision we make, it will be the wrong one. A mistake, as you know, should never be looked upon as a time or place of inertia but rather as one of training. Mistakes are opportunities to evaluate what is and isn't working in your current system of beliefs and convictions. Once you acknowledge that though you've made a mistake, realize there are lessons to be learned that will help you to gain a stronger alignment with your inner self.

Being at peace with your present life means knowing what is and isn't best for you and declaring: "I will not allow anything or anyone into my life that will cause an unwanted change." Being at peace for me means that I accept myself for the woman I have become, I accept the life I have created for myself. With the wisdom of my past and the knowledge of my future, I bring tranquility to my here and now. With this mind-set, you will not be easily wavered in your convictions about what is right and truth for you. When your approach to life is one of certainty and confidence, alignment becomes uncomplicated. You are able to see clearly the path you are destined to trod and experience life the way you chose. Decisions become easier for you because now you only make decisions and commitments that are in alignment with your inner convictions.

As adults, we recognize that wherever we are in life today is a direct reflection of the decisions we've made yesterday. And as a result, we can agree that the decisions we make today will have an impact on how we live tomorrow. Therefore, in order to have peace concerning our future, we must bring into alignment our behaviors and convictions today to ensure that our future is one that we desire.

Our journey to Awaken the Woman Within will always begin with a decision: a decision to remain consistent with our beliefs and convictions that will bring honor and respect to families, our communities and ourselves. Be adamant and resolute in aligning your outer behaviors with your inner convictions. Determine that you will not surrender to activities and manners that do not reflect woman you are within. There are times when doing what is right may seem to be most difficult choice, but it is during these complex times that it is most important for us to adhere to the truth that makes us who we are.

What is truth for you? What do you believe to be the standard of living that you must maintain for yourself? How would others rate your character? Can others determine your inner convictions by the life they see you live? Ask yourself these questions and with honest answers, determine if you are being authentic to yourself and to the woman within. Form an alignment now by resolving that you will not be double minded, but that you will live a life that is worthy of respect, admiration and honor for living what you speaking and speaking what you live.

Principles to Remember

I. Determination and resiliency have to be cultivated from within to have the strength not to acquiesce to your surroundings.

II. As we listen to the power and truth within, we gain immeasurable lessons about our self-esteem, our self-value and our self-worth.

III. Never shrink yourself so that others will feel comfortable around you.

IV. Aligning our outer behaviors with our inner convictions sends a message to those around us that we are worthy of respect.

Principle Four: Believe In Your Potential

It is a fact that everything in life has potential. The apple has within itself apple seeds to grow apple trees; hence in every seed, there is a tree. In every tree there lies a forest. In every boy, there is a man and in every girl there is a woman. It is easy to see that everything God created possesses potential.

Potential is one of those words we often hear. Not only do we hear our teachers, mentors, and pastors speak of potential, but we often find ourselves, rehearsing the phrase, "I know I have the potential to accomplish this task." But what is potential? I know we use the word in our everyday language, but its one of those words that I had to sit down and study.

In my study, I found that potential is really having the ability to become something that you have not yet become. Potential is what you can do, but have not done yet. It knows that you can reach the distance, but have not yet arrived. Potential can be defined as knowing that you are capable of achieving, yet you have not achieved.

I like what Dr. Miles Monroe says, "Potential is… dormant ability… reserved power… untapped strength… unused success… hidden talents… capped capability."

My definition: potential is knowing that you have the ability and capacity of doing and being more than you are now.

Keeping this definition in mind, we realize that our potential is not in what we have accomplished but what we have yet to accomplish.

Never be satisfied by what you have accomplished. Though we should always celebrate our successes, we should never become complacent in our achievements. Success sometimes can be the greatest killer of potential. I say this because some of us feel that we have nothing else to work for after we have attained our goals. But it is at this time that we are to continuing growing by developing new goals and new strategies that will challenge us to live up to our full potential. The minute we begin to settle is the minute we begin to lose the potential of what's really on the inside of us.

Born For Greatness

You are more than you think you are; you are more than you seem. God sees so much more in you than you will ever see in yourself. When God created us, He placed within all of us a potential for greatness. Whether you believe it or not, there is greatness inside of you. The sad part is that there is only a small percentage of people in the entire world who will ever live up to the measure of their true potential. It is sad to know that so many great men and women will die with untapped potential. They will die and they will take with them bestselling books, number one songs, multi-million dollars businesses, cures for diseases and many more gifts to the world all because they didn't believe in their potential.

One of my personal commitments to life is to "die empty." When I die, I do not want to take anything with me. Every book God has placed within me, every smile or hug I was supposed to give and every lesson I was supposed to teach, I don't want to take it with me, but rather, I want to "die empty" hence maximizing all of the potential that God has placed within me.

Can you imagine what life would be life if Martin Luther King, Jr. never believed in his potential? What about Bill Gates? Can you imagine our lives today without streetlights? Or what about your local place of worship? How different would your life have been if your leaders had not believed in what God placed within them?

This one is a hard to imagine, but what if your mother died before birthing you? What would the world be missing out on if you were not here? Your smile, your love, your gifts and talents, your contributions to your community, we would all be missing out on the contributions that you have to give had you not been born. The good news is that you are here and alive. And an even better thing is that the world is waiting on you to fulfill your entire God given potential. We are waiting on you to be the next inspirational speaker, children's author, politician, interior designer, photographer, surgeon or singer. We will never be blessed to receive what you never first believe yourself to possess.

Do you believe you are living your life to its fullest? Do you believe that God placed authentic valuables within you for so that you can benefit the world ? Whether you believe it or not, the answer is yes, and we will never know what God has placed within us until we begin the journey within. Once we begin excavating our authentic selves, we will find what has been planted there the entire time: the potential for greatness.

Belief Busters

There are some situations we experience that can zap out the belief we have in ourselves right away.

All my life I have believed that I was to be a national speaker. It was prophesied to me as a child and with childlike faith, I believed what I heard. God began to show me in visions and dreams the future that was in store for me. I believed with all of my heart that a life of a great speaker would be mine one day.

Before I knew I wanted to be a speaker, I knew I wanted to be in the limelight. In junior high school, I was in show choir, in high school I participated in musicals; year after year I was involved in speech contests and anything that had to do with entertaining an audience. What I didn't know then was that I had a passion to give- to give inspiration and hope to people by using the gifts and talents that God gave me. I couldn't articulate it then, all I knew was that I wanted to make other people feel good about themselves, and whether I could do that by singing a song or playing a dramatic role in a play, I knew I wanted to make people smile.

Then came the call of God to ministry. Scared and unaware of my purpose, I trusted what God told me. He gave me comfort by speaking to me the words of the Prophet Ezekiel out of the third chapter of the Book of Ezekiel. Determined to please God, I began living a life of total consecration and dedication to Him. At the young age of 15, I made a vow to God that if He would stay with me that I would be His oracle and servant for the rest of my life.

While God held up His end of the promise, I broke mine. In my mid twenties I got pregnant. Embarrassed for my family, my church and myself I turned my back on God and everything that I knew to be true for myself. I turned to a life of riotous living, a life I'd never known and never wanted to know. I found myself developing into the very person that I taught women across the country not to be. It was a hard road for me, one that I will never forget and one that I will always appreciate.

It was during this time that I began to feel that it was all over for me. All the dreams, visions, prophecies and prayers were null and void because my sins separated me from God. I know now that God was never separated from me, but it was my sinfulness that separated me from God.

I began to see on Christian television many of my friends whom I knew and had started with in the ministry. I watched as they continued to move forward in their lives. I watched number one albums, bestselling books and I watched as some of this nation's greatest preachers mounted platforms.

As I watched from afar, I began to ask the God, "Is it over for me? Have I really blown it?" For what seemed like an eternity there was never an answer. I never really heard the voice of the Lord speaking to me during this season. Although there was no answer, God remained sovereign in His silence.

All of my hope and faith was gone. No longer did I believe in the words the Lord had spoken to me. For this time, what I believed was that restoration would never take place and that I had just missed my appointment with destiny.

It is in these times of hardship and what some might call failure that we come to know God for who He really is. Not only do we come to know God, but also we come to know and understand ourselves. I let my situation convince me that all God had placed within me, all of His promises and potential, He had taken back.

Today my joy is in knowing one of the promises of God is that whatever He has started in you, not only will He complete it, but also He will perfect everything that concerns you (Ps 138:8). I found joy in knowing that when I stopped believing in myself, God never stopped believing in me. How could He, when He knows everything He placed within in me and no matter what the detour, He would be waiting for me once I found the path back to His house?

In my mother's womb God knew I would get pregnant before I got married. He knew that I would take the path I took in ignorance and fear. He also knew that I would stop believing in my dreams and potential because of my sins.

These "Belief Busters" zap us from everything we know to be true for our lives. Call them what you like: detours, wrong exits, pit stops, mistakes or failures, they can all zap our belief in what God has told us throughout over our lives. The good news is that we do not have to succumb to them. And by the grace and mercy of God we are able to continue with His original assignment for our lives.

Living the Thoughts of God

I have learned many lessons in my lifetime, but there is one lesson I think is imperative to share with you in this chapter. That lesson is this: Just because your path changes, God's assignment for your life doesn't change. The way God originally intended for you to travel may be altered by your lack of discipline, lack of focus or just outright laziness, but the truth is that our God is a God that changes not. The words and promises that He spoke concerning your life will never fall to the ground or return to Him void (Isaiah 55:11). They must all come to pass.

It is easy to stop believing in yourself when you feel like you are staring hell right in the face. It's easy to see the potential in everyone else while you stand on the sideline like a cheerleader. But I want to encourage you to never stop believing.

Never stop believing in what you know God intends for you. The book of Jeremiah says that God knows the thoughts that He has for us, thoughts of good and not evil, to give us an expected end (Jeremiah 29:11). My purpose in life now is to live the thoughts of God. I want to do this for myself and for my life. If He thought it then it must be good, it must have purpose and it must have meaning. It is in the heart of God above all that we prosper and live to our full potential.

It's not about what you should have done, or what you could have done, but it is about what you are going to do. Let go of your yesterday because it is only a memory. Begin today with a list of lost projects, lost ideas, lost purposes and visions that you know you are to fulfill. Begin living your life today as if God is behind you every step of the way to ensure that you live life to the fullest, because He is.

I know there was a point in my life where I just couldn't muster up enough belief and faith in myself to achieve anything. It seemed as if everyone else around me saw my potential. My friends and mentors all said that they could see greatness in me, but I couldn't see it for myself. I learned that it is in times like these when we cannot believe in ourselves that we have to believe in someone else's belief in us until our own belief kicks in.

I thank God for my mentors and the leaders who never stopped believing in me. Even when I had people tell me I would never preach again, the love and support of my mentors gave me the strength I needed to keep on moving.

I didn't believe I had it in me, but they did and that was enough for me. I believed in their belief in me and after a while, my own belief kicked in.

It isn't an easy road, but you can make it. Nothing in life worth having is worth giving up on. Never give up on yourself, never let go of your dreams and never doubt your potential. You are more than you think you are- you are more than what you seem.

Open the eyes of your heart and see yourself as God sees you- a woman of purpose- a woman of power- a woman of potential. The world is waiting for you to bless us with your gifts. Always remember that your life is God's gift to you, what you do with your life is your gift to God.

Conquer the Limitations Others Put on You

The times we find it most difficult to believe in our own potential is when those closest to us place limitations on our ability to succeed. Whether the limitation is placed because of what appears to be lack of physical ability or personal knowledge or skill level, it never feels good to be doubted by those you love.

King David can attest to that. Family and friends may place limitations on you based off of what they see, but God looks at the heart while man sees only the outward appearance (I Sam 16:6-7). Through the story of King David, we can find reason to believe in our personal potential and greatness when all odds are against us.

Many images come to mind when we think of King David, but we don't think of him as someone who had to overcome the limitations of others. David was the greatest king and warrior of his time. Anointed by Samuel to be king while still a young boy, he found early on that the greatest struggles would be with those who tried to put limitations on him. Although he was chosen by God to be the next king, he did not receive encouragement from those around him or support in his plight for destiny.

Because of his age and size, his father, Jesse, didn't deem him fit to be the next king. When Samuel announced that God had chosen one of his sons to be anointed king, Jesse found Eliab, his oldest son to be the appropriate choice. Likewise, the prophet Samuel also thought that Eliab was to be the next king of Israel. But as Samuel and Jesse were looking at the outward appearance, God was looking at the heart. God wanted David. He wanted the son with heart. Let us learn from the story of David that God will value us for who we are even when our surroundings don't.

Not only did David experience rejection from his father, but from his brothers as well. As far as they could see, the only place that David served was tending to the sheep. They looked at him as an errand boy who served no other purpose than to care for his father's flock. They despised the fact that Jesse questioned the soldiers' fear of Goliath when he was sent to bring food to the battle line during the war with the Philistines (I Sam 17:28). Though David's family saw him only as a Shepard boy, he was really a man with a mission.

When word got to King Saul that there was someone who wondered why everyone feared Goliath and was stating that he would be willing to fight, he summonsed him to his court. When David came before the king, a ruddy fellow as the Bible describes him, Saul looking at the stature and age of David said to him, "You are not able to go against this Philistine to fight with him." Saul was confidant that David was not warrior material and insisted that he wore his royal armor (See I Sam 17: 32-33). Of course, Saul's armor, fit for a mature warrior, would not fit David's youthful figure. It was the wisdom of David that didn't allow him to be hinder by the armor. Instead he decided to go and fight Goliath with what he had.

Saul tried to make David become someone he wasn't. David had enough courage to say, I will not use your armor, but I will go in the strength of the Lord. Saul wanted David to fight the battle as he would, with his armor, but God wanted David to be himself. Likewise, God is looking for you to be your authentic self even when some people around you wants you to handle situations the way they would. Dare to be different and be the person that only you can be.

We learn from David that we have to throw off the limitations set on us by others. It is easy for others to write us off as failures or of little importance. But when God has anointed you for a task, there isn't any limitation that will hinder His will from being fulfilled.

The story of David teaches us that we can always determine the level of greatness that rests on someone's life by the level of opposition they receive. Show me someone great and I'll show you someone who has received major resistance on his or her path to destiny.

Decide today to be one of the few people who not only acknowledge their potential but who also decide to maximize the potential given to them by God. I challenge you to be one of the few who will chart an uncharted path, one of the few who will blaze the trail for many to follow. Do something that has never been done, answer the call to authenticity, dare to believe in your potential. You will never regret that you did.

Birthing Your Potential

Several years ago I became pregnant with my daughter Imani Marie. Scared and unprepared, I felt I didn't have the ability to raise a child the way I knew one should be raised. At the time, I was still very young, immature and irresponsible. "How am I," I would ask myself, "going to raise a child?" Thoughts of inadequacy quickly filled my head and heart as I would reflect on how unfit I was. With no friends to lean on and no husband to share the responsibility, I turned to my mother. My mother, one of the most strongest and powerful women I have ever met, spoke words of comfort to me and told me that it is during times like these that the woman within you will rise to the occasion. She assured me that I had every quality needed to be a good mother, and that although I'd never seen or displayed these qualities before that at the right time they would manifest. I decided to believe my mother; after all, she raised me alone while she was very young.

She was right. Although I had, and still have, room for improvement in the motherhood department, it remains true that everything I needed to care for my child came to the forefront when I grasped the fact that this was a human being who totally depended on me. Her very life and existence, her support and supply had to come from me. I had no option but to become the mother she needed. With no alternative options, I had to awaken myself to motherhood.

Single motherhood anointed me. It gave me an anointing to care, love and protect in ways that I've never known. There is an anointing that comes with single motherhood that forces you to do what is right, not just for today, but for the future. A single mother realizes that her previous ways and habits are no longer acceptable. There is a child to protect, and she will do everything within her power to ensure that that child isn't exposed to any negative influences, people or situations that will cause her harm. There is an anointing that comes with single motherhood that forces you to become a positive example. Even when you don't want to or don't feel like it, the fact that you have given birth to this child, propels you to do what is in his or her best interest.

As with motherhood, we sometimes feel unequipped to birth the potential that God has given us. Whether we like it or not, we know that we have been blessed with gifts and talents that are undeniable, but it seems as if we do not have the capacity to nurture, develop and cultivate these gifts. Like a child, your gifts and talents must be protected, they must be tended to and they must be cared for. For something to grow successfully, it has to be placed in the proper environment. If you want to see your ability to write lyrics, you cannot write once a month or every other week, but as often as you hear the words ringing within your spirit, you must take pen to paper and allow the words to flow.

This is how we birth our potential. Day in and day out we must take the necessary steps that will allow us to move forward, grow and cultivate our potential. It will not grow on its own, it must be directed and guided and the only person to do this is you. Your potential cannot grow and develop alone; it is going to take the hard work, discipline and dedication to birth it out to its full stages of development.

When God created you to be a woman, He not only meant for you to be a mother but also a mother of your destiny, of your today and tomorrow by birthing out your potential.

Becoming the birth mother to your potential requires that you give of yourself to yourself. It takes time for nurturing and patience. As with natural birth, you have to give time to gestation. This is the season that God will plant ideas, insights, power and possibilities within you. There will always be a time between sowing and reaping, between pregnancy and delivery. During this time, allow God to speak to you through His word by spending quiet time with Him. Allow daily time for devotion and mediation as He gives you the instructions needed for your assignment. Be careful what you expose yourself to during this time, allow your spirit and mind to remain untainted from ideas and concepts that will harm the seed of your potential.

Remember that you are the birth mother of your potential, your possibilities and your destiny. In the natural world, a mother must be careful about her diet. While a woman is pregnant, she has to stay conscious of her exercise, her weight and the amount of rest she receives. It is imperative that she adjusts her daily routine to accommodate the growth and changes of the baby. So too must a spiritual birth mother adjust her life to ensure her destiny reaches full term. You may not realize it now, but God is birthing within you abilities you've never imagined. God wants you to know that you are capable of carrying and growing your potential.

If you've ever given birth, or perhaps if you know someone who has, you know what it's like to be pregnant for the first time. There is the nausea, fatigue, morning sickness and swollen ankles. Everyone knows that giving birth is hard on the mind, the body and the emotions. Pregnancy can be especially hard on the body; the weight of the growing baby inside often leaves behind stretch marks.

We often see the stretch marks of life as we carry within us the child of destiny. The stress and strain of life both internally and externally will work both our bodies and spirits overtime.

Just as in the natural, we must remember that the stretch marks are an indication that we have the ability to expand when the pressure is added. As we are carrying our potential, we must remember that we have the capacity to handle growth and change. Your stretch marks show that you have the ability to expand to new responsibilities.

Although the stretch marks can leave behind unwanted marks on our bodies, they are a reminder that we have what it takes to be a birth mother. Let us learn how to embrace our marks, as they give us the sign that we have the ability to grow, nurture and birth our potential with the help of God.

All Things Are Possible to Those Who Believe

You have what it takes to succeed. You have what it takes to accomplish every goal, desire, dream or ambition within you- but you must first believe. As we embark on this journey together to Awaken The Woman Within, let us remember that belief in self, above all else, is the most important principle to developing your authentic self. Starting your journey with a positive belief system will give you the courage and strength needed to continue your pursuit when all odds are against you. Belief in your potential, your purpose and your power will forge an alliance within you that will awaken you to your higher self.

Nothing shall be impossible to you if you believe. Be guided not by what you see, but by what you believe. Let nothing lead you astray from what you know is true for yourself, your journey and your purpose. Believe that with God, all things are possible, because they are. Believe that nothing that comes against you can stop you, because it can't. Believe that within you lies every thing that you need to overcome, achieve and succeed, because it is.

Believe. When all else fails, never stop believing. And when you feel like your belief is failing you, ask God to "Help thou my unbelief." He's there, waiting to take you up on eagle wings, to give you the strength you need to continue believing. Believe.

Principles to Remember

I. Potential is knowing that you have the ability and capacity of doing and being more than you are now.

II. Whether you believe it or not, there is greatness inside of you.

III. Just because your path changes, God's assignment for your life doesn't change.

IV. Remember that you are the birth mother of your potential, your possibilities and your destiny.

Principle Five: Honor Your Worthiness to Achieve

In order to become awakened, literally coming to know your very purpose for existing, you must first know that you are worthy of achieving. This means that you will have to review and examine some attitudes and beliefs that you hold about yourself. Your perception, the lens through which you see yourself, is the foundation for what you want to examine.

Awakening involves looking inward to find, know and understand your authentic voice. It involves using your inner spirit to create the life and relationships you desire. You can remind yourself all day long that there is a woman inside you who is ready to come forth, but if you do not feel worthy, you will hinder the natural flow of manifesting your destiny and make achievement for yourself impossible.

The fifth principle reminds you that you are worthy of success. If you allow your mind to meditate on subjects that speak to your unworthiness, you will cause those thoughts to manifest into your everyday life. The truths found in the fourth principle will align with what you accept as truth in the fifth principle. Always remember, "As a man thinketh, so is he," are not just words of a parable, but also words to live by, they state a basic truth of how the awakening journey works.

Thinking that achievement is unattainable is an untruth that influences many of us and is one of the largest obstacles there is to feeling worthy.

Low self-esteem and low self-worth conceived in us since childbirth fuel the myth that one who desires to have and achieve greatness in life is prideful. It is important for us as we journey to Awaken the Woman Within to determine if we are influenced by this myth.

Take time to look around you and notice the quantity of people who are operating at a level they have created for themselves by the perception they have of themselves. To say that one can obtain abundance and prosperity without believing they are first worthy to receive is an untruth. All that you see first began with a thought: a thought of worthiness to receive abundance or a thought of unworthiness to receive. But it all began with a thought. Make no mistakes about it, you are what you think and you will have whatever you believe to be true for yourself.

There is no reason to feel ashamed of wanting blessings and abundance to come into your life. It is better to have an attitude of deserving than an attitude of accepting whatever comes into your life. We remove the myth of pride and selfishness when we realize that God only wants what is best for us, so as He desires for me to have the best, so too should I desire that I achieve and receive all that belongs to me. Do not allow the thoughts of selfishness set in as you begin to desire achievement for yourself. Just as each of us have been given an assignment by God, so too have we all been given our measure of blessings and abundance. It's yours for the asking and you are worthy to receive it.

Everything that we need to overcome to make this fifth principle true for our lives is available to us through our inner spirit. You do not need to go out and get opinions and ask advice from others, but rather turn inward to listen to the woman within. Allow her to change your mind about your worthiness to receive the blessings of God.

Our society has made it so that we have automatically conditioned ourselves to feel unworthy of having all life has to offer and achieving all that we are able to achieve. Most of us have accepted a lot of these untruths. Whether we feel worthy or unworthy of the blessings of God is a direct reflection of our inner self. In order to remove the stigma of unworthiness, we will need to rearrange our inner perceptions. There are core components to honoring your worthiness to achieve. The following are perceptions that you must have of yourself as you Awaken the Woman Within and Honor Your Worthiness to Achieve. They are tools needed for creating an inner atmosphere of worthiness.

Self-acceptance. Self-love. Self-confidence. Self-respect. Self-esteem. All are necessary ingredients for a centered and grounded woman. They are the attributes that open the door to an abundant life. They become the bricks on which we build a solid foundation for growth and empowerment. They help determine how effective and consistent we live our lives.

We have been taught from our youth the importance of self-love and self-respect. We know on a very deep and personal level that we must first love ourselves before we are able to give love to others. Our mothers, teachers and mentors have taught us the value of self-respect; reminding us to treat ourselves as someone worthy of respect and demand that everyone else treat us the same. But we often have difficulty embracing this self-centered, self-admiration. We find it easier, we think, to love, respect, and embrace others first, while we ourselves remain empty and receptive to whatever love and attention is given to us by others.

We find it hard as women, to put ourselves first. This is partially because of some cultural teaching that says in order to be an effective parent, mother, provider, guardian or caretaker, you must put the needs of others before your own. I'm under the persuasion that if we do not take care of ourselves, we will never be in the position to take care of others. Think of the oxygen mask principle we're taught when we fly on an airplane. In case of an emergency, all adults should place their facemask on first and then place the facemask on the child. It isn't because we're to be so selfish and that we want to ensure safety for ourselves only, but rather we want to be certain that we are taken care of so that we can be of help to the child.

It is true that when we do not satisfy our physical, mental and spiritual need for self-appreciation, we become stagnant in every area of our lives. It is at this time that the woman within begins to whisper to us that it is time for retreat, a sabbatical and a time to reflect. The woman within never yells; she always whispers and awaits our respond. As we take time to stop and reflect, we realize how important and necessary these sabbaticals really are.

You Deserve To Achieve

Some time ago, just after I'd completely forgiven myself for becoming pregnant with my daughter, Imani Marie, an astonishing depression took over me. I couldn't figure out why I was so down in the dumps. God had forgiven me of my sins and He'd showed me His mercy and forgiveness by allowing me the opportunity to feel the embrace of His never-failing love. The Lord gave plenty of provisions for my child and me, affording me the ability to work for a company that sufficed our needs. Again, the ministry assignments began to come my way again as well. It should have been a great time in my life. Although a lot of people didn't think it fitting that I should again be allowed to minister the gospel of Jesus Christ after becoming pregnant out of wedlock, God had something else in mind. God believed in me and He put me back in my place in Him. Finally, I was at peace with my past, my mistakes and myself. I could attend church without the shame of feeling as though everyone was staring at me, thinking inwardly how hypocritical I was. I was on track for repairing my credit, my bills were paid and Imani and I were at the beginning stages of building a great life.

So what could have been so wrong? Why could I not stop crying? Why did I have feelings of unworthiness, disconnection and unhappiness? One evening before retiring, I lay in bed asking the Spirit to help me understand my unexplainable feelings. As I lay there, I began to understand that even though I had forgiven myself, I really didn't feel as though I deserved any of the blessings and achievements God was allowing me to receive. So that night, for the first time, I got out of my bed, walked into the bathroom, looked myself in the mirror and said to myself, "You deserve to achieve."

It was at that moment that I realized that even though I had forgiven myself, there was a large part of me that continued to feel as though I was a failure and that I wasn't worthy of achievement. For so long I had been trying to prove to others that I was worthy of a second chance- that I deserved another shot at life, at a chance to begin again. I realized that all of my energy had been focused on other people, on proving to them that I did belong. In an instant I saw what was happening to me: although outwardly I began to move forward, inwardly I was living in stagnation. The disconnection I felt inside was a result of my feelings of unworthiness.

Although we talk a lot about self-love and true happiness, it seems very few of us are able to find the power within to believe that we really deserve it. Some of us find it very difficult to practice self-love and true happiness in a very real way. I realized that day that I did deserve happiness and that no matter how it appeared to others, I would honor myself as someone worthy of achievement. I felt at peace with myself and with my life. I knew that in order to continue on this path that I would have to remind myself to retreat regularly, to take time to speak words of life and encouragement to my spirit, to allow time for personal healing.

Though daily we come to God with humble reverence and fear, we must also remember that we are to make honoring ourselves and our achievements through the power of God part of our sacred time. Remember to congratulate yourself for making it through one more day, and for accomplishing the many tasks that were before you. Only you know what an arduous task it can be to get through each day and as you do, with the help of God, make honoring yourself a part of each one.

Make a commit today to begin honoring yourself for the things that you do. Honoring and loving yourself makes it easier for you to get up and work out in the morning. When you begin to love and appreciate yourself, it becomes easy for you to say no to the things that you know will cause harm to yourself. Pushing the plate back becomes easier when you know that you are a beautiful vessel worthy of the love that can come only from God and yourself.

Honoring yourself will make it easier to make wise decisions. You no longer have to contemplate starting your new business, writing your book or going back to school to finish your degree, because you know that you are worthy of nothing but the best. This new respect and love for ourselves makes it easier to save money for a new house, it gives us the discipline we need to sacrifice a pair of shoes to save for the future of our lives. Affirming who you are reminds you that there is purpose and destiny for your life and that you are not just here for yourself, but to make a positive impact in the lives of others.

The feeling of self-love I felt that memorable evening was a starting point in my life. I learned that loving ourselves must be a continuous commitment. We are not meant to wait for permission from others to honor ourselves; the honor must begin with the woman within. There we find the ability to nurture, renew and embrace our true selves. And in doing so, we begin to live a life that places us on a path to fulfilling our true destiny.

Principles to Remember

I. Awakening involves looking inward to find, know and understand your authentic voice.

II. If you allow your mind to meditate on subjects that speak to your unworthiness, you will cause those thoughts to manifest into your everyday life.

III. Remember to congratulate yourself for making it through one more day, and for accomplishing the many tasks that were before you.

IV. Honoring yourself will make it easier to make wise decisions

Principle Six: Trust Yourself First

If you are like me, you've made a lot of bad decisions in your life. Some decisions may have been well thought out, while others were just a spur of the moment. Either way, the majority of the decisions you make turn out to be less than perfect. You think you are doing what is right at the time, only to realize in hindsight that it was the worst thing you could have done.

You're not alone. We all make bad decisions, some more than others, but we all do. Whether big or small, the point is that there are times when we really find ourselves making a mess out of our lives. Decision upon decision, we continue to put ourselves in worse shape than before. The sad part is that you would think that we would learn from our past decision making mistakes and change. But out of habit, it seems to be a vicious cycle, one that if not dwelt with properly can lead to intense regret and ultimately depression. There are times when we have to make bad decisions in order to grow. There are some of us who, no matter how much guidance we receive, we have to try it out and decide for ourselves only to find out that the advice we were given in the first place was correct.

One of the greatest downfalls of continuously making bad decisions is that poor decision-making alters your faith in yourself. Your faith in your ability to decide what is right concerning your life is minimal; hence causing a domino effect of bad decision making skills, creating a greater level of insecurity and inadequacy.

Once you begin to feel as though you're not sure what is right for yourself, your life or the lives of your children, you develop an instinct to look outward for advice, direction, counsel and faith. When we are unable to trust ourselves, we falter in confidence and begin only trusting in others. We lack the self-assurance that is necessary to ensure ourselves that we know what is right for our lives.

The truth of the matter is that we always know what is right. We have an inner witness, an inner voice, a woman within that is always speaking to us. The Bible teaches us that the Holy Spirit has come to be our Teacher, and that He would teach and guide us into all truth. Believing this will afford us the comfort in knowing that the Truth and Wisdom of what we should do in every situation is within us.

Trusting ourselves after what seems like continued failure sometimes seems impossible. I know this is true for me. Several years ago, I went through a phase in my life where I just made a series of bad decisions. One after another, decision after decision, I'd always seemed to do just the opposite of what I should have done. I would take time and reflect and say, "the next time, I will think things through before I decide." But time and time again, anxiously and impatiently, I'd do what felt right for the moment.

I can remember a time when I made a minor decision regarding a housing situation. I called several people to get their opinions. Upon listening to my friend's advice, I called one more friend. I informed them of the situation, told them that I'd spoken with other individuals as well and just wondered what their thoughts were on what I should do. They rendered some advice and said they hoped everything worked out for me.

Several moments later, my phone rung from the same person, calling to share something with me. They wanted me to know that I was a very intelligent woman. That I was capable of making my own decisions and that I didn't need the advice or opinions of five of my friends to determine what was right for me. They reminded me that I had all of the ability and knowledge I needed to do what was right. Then they said something that I will never forget. In a compassionate tone they noted that it was obvious that I'd made some bad mistakes in my past and that I was now paying the consequences for the mistakes. But they ensured me that the mistakes I'd made were not going to handicap me for the future, but would prepare me to make more informed and intelligent decisions.

I was reminded that it is okay to ask for advice, but to never forget to trust myself first, that the decisions I needed to make I was capable of making on my own.

I will never forget that conversation. I still become emotional every time I think about. I know it is because that has always been a very sensitive area in my life. Something of which I never spoke of with anyone nor has anyone ever addressed the issue with me.

The truth is that I didn't trust myself. I forgot how to trust myself, or better yet, I don't think I ever knew how to trust myself. I always felt that someone else knew what was better for me. Over and over again, I called my best friend to ask her what she thought. I tried to find an answer in a book or on the Internet, anything other than trusting myself first.

Trusting yourself first is an authentic principle that must be cultivated by faith in God and yourself. You must have faith in God to believe that in every situation He will direct your path. Your faith in God has to increase to a level of total obedience to Him regardless what the situation may be. Trusting yourself stems from trusting God foremost, knowing that He will never lead you astray and that His thoughts and intentions for you are always good and never evil. Your faith level will increase as you obey the voice of the Lord and begin seeing the fruit of your obedience.

A Hearing Ear

I've recently experienced a very traumatic adventure. I purchased a new car after being without one for several months. Less than 24 hours after the vehicle was off the car lot, it was stolen. In shock, I was numb and speechless. After crying profusely, I contacted the authorities to file an official police report. I was told that it would be several hours before an officer could come to the scene and that I would have better luck if someone drove me to the police station.

Upon arriving at the police station, I was informed that because I did not have the tag number to the vehicle that I would not be able to file a report. I could show nothing that stated that the car actually belong to me. I informed the authorities that I'd just purchased the vehicle the night before and it never crossed my mind to notate the tag number.

I was advised that there was nothing they could do to help me at the time and that I could come back the next day after I found out the tag number. I stood there with tears rolling down my face in utter disbelief. I bowed my head in the middle of the police station and said, "Father, this sounds like a job for you."

Once I left the police station and back in my friend's car, I sat in the passenger side praying in my spirit asking God what was the reason for this extreme situation. In the midst of my prayer, I felt my faith kick in and I asked my friend who was driving if I could drive. I told her that I felt as though I could find the car myself. I prayed and said to God, "God, if I am your prophet, I ask that you show me where my car is." Unbeknownst to me was the fact that I was a few miles away from the car.

My prayer has always been that God would give me a hearing ear, a hearing ear to hear His voice, to hear His instructions and to heed His command. I needed to hear Him more than ever that day and hear Him I did. While I was yet asking God to lead me to the car, I heard His voice speaking to me, telling me which way to turn and what street to take. In less than five minutes, I drove directly to my car. With my heart racing and my spirit rejoicing I knew that it was only God who could have done such a thing.

Trusting God and trusting ourselves is never easy. It takes time, experience and persistence. I use the word persistence because only with the consistent hearing and obeying the voice of the Lord will you come to know what He desires for you.

I like to use the example of talking on the telephone to a new friend. In the beginning of any relationship it is always necessary to identify yourself when making telephone calls. This is due partially to the fact that you and your new friend are not acclimated to each other, unsure of the other's voice. But over time, after speaking in person and on the telephone on a daily and weekly basis, your voices become familiar and the need to identify yourself is no longer needed.

Such is true with knowing the voice of the Lord. Once you begin to speak and listen to Him on a daily basis, His voice becomes distinguishable to you and without question, you know when He is and isn't speaking to you.

It is because of our personal relationship with God, with knowing His voice that we are able to Trust Ourselves First. We can trust ourselves because we rest in the assurance that We Hear God. And in hearing God we know that the One who knows all and who sees all is directing our steps, our decisions and our choices.

Cultivating a personal relationship with God that will yield a hearing ear and faith in knowing that our steps are ordered by Him teaches us how to Trust Ourselves First. This is a lesson we must all learn in order to have both natural and spiritual success. As we learn to look and listen inward through prayer and mediation we find an inner peace that brings us both comfort and serenity. I find that I am my best self when I am in constant prayer and mediation. Finding time daily to meet with God, to hear from Him and to know His plans for my life gives me certainty needed to take life on with everything I've got.

Principles to Remember

I. When we are unable to trust ourselves, we falter in confidence and begin only trusting in others.

II. Trusting yourself first is an authentic principle that must be cultivated by faith in God and yourself.

III. We can trust ourselves because we rest in the assurance that We Hear God.

IV. Cultivating a personal relationship with God that will yield a hearing ear and faith in knowing that our steps are ordered by Him teaches us how to Trust Ourselves First.

Principle Seven: Identify and Conquer Your Insecurities

All of us have experienced some form of insecurity. Whether it was a public or private matter, we have all suffered at some point of an insecurity that has made our personal relationships and interpersonal communications difficult for both others and ourselves.

The main objective in this chapter is to address the internal struggles we have as women. As women, some of us find it hard to share with even our closest friends our feelings of inadequacies and low self-worth. Whether it is because of our education or skill level or because of a perceived lack of physical fitness or outward beauty, we sometimes feel that compared to others we will never measure up.

Like many women, I suffered from low self-esteem and feelings of underachievement and unattractiveness for most of my life. I can say that these feelings are part of my earliest memories. For the longest time, I'd felt as though every one of my friends was prettier than me. That no matter what I'd do, I would never be as pretty as them. In high school, no matter how hard I'd try, I could never get my Grade Point Average to surpass my friends. And looking back, I know it didn't help that while all the other girls were talking about their new bras, I kept silent, because as I am today, so I was then flat chest.

It can be hard growing up as a young girl. It doesn't matter if you are White, Asian, Latino, Black or Hispanic, it is tough growing up as a girl. Kids are cruel. We'd tease each other about things that we knew no one had control over. I couldn't control the fact that I had flat chest and a big nose. It really wasn't my fault that I was skinny as a rail. But growing up as a child, you feel it is your fault, and unfortunately those feelings of inadequacy don't end at puberty, but continue to be a part of our adult life. They follow us into interviews, meetings with superiors and conversations with colleagues, these memories are reminders that we may not measure up to the person in front of us.

I send blessings to my sisters who are reading this chapter and may not be able to relate. It could be that some of you have always had a healthy dose of self-esteem and things just didn't seem that bad for you growing up. I am glad that is your testimony. Unfortunately for some of us, growing up with issues and insecurities just wasn't as easy.

It's taken a while, but I finally got it. I finally realized that I am perfect and beautiful just the way I am. I realized after years of feeling sending hateful messages to myself by my thoughts and actions, that there will never be another me, that I am one of a kind, and that I am wonderfully made by God (Psalms 139:14). I realized my high cheekbones and wide nose are a part of my Cherokee Indian heritage- something to be proud of.

I've never been so in love with myself as I am now. With the revelation that I am Azizah, as my mother named me, full of might and majesty, able to enforce myself with dignity. This is who I am, this is who I have always been, and this is who God made me to be. I am The King's Daughter, I am His Servant, I am His Minister, I am an Encourager, an Evangelist and I am an Inspirational Speaker, Author, Mentor, Mother and Friend. This is who I am, with all of my flaws, issues and mistakes; I have awakened the woman within and this is who she is.

God Has a Place for You

Who is the woman that God created you to be? Is she still hiding behind the fears of her youth? Is she still hiding behind the mask of uncertainty? Are you behind where you should be in your life and can't figure out why you can't move forward? If so, part of the answer is to identify those things that have hindered your growth and progression. What could it be?

For example, does your stagnation stem from being adopted as a child? Have you always felt as though you would never be or was never loved because you are an adoptee? If so, have you considered Queen Esther?

In Queen Esther we find a woman who had a great sense of purpose and destiny. Though for many years she did not have this resiliency. She did not know in the beginning, that God had a place for her. Like you and I, she was uncertain about her future because of her past. Esther's parents died when she was a young girl and so her uncle Mordecai adopted her. Living in a strange land, she felt out of place, as though she didn't belong.

Have you ever felt as though you didn't belong? Most people have felt that way. There are times when we don't feel the sense of community we would like to feel with others. At times we feel as though we are too inadequate to accomplish assignments given to us. At other times we just seem to feel isolated from our surroundings- we simply feel out of place. This is something that Esther can relate to because for years she felt out of place, like she just didn't belong. All of her life she was removed from her family, culture and country. But the story of Esther so beautifully reminds us that you are never out of place when you are in place with God.

Esther did not know that God had uniquely placed her in the King's Court to be the deliver for her people. She did not know that her being in the King's Court was not only about her but also about an entire nation. How so can we relate? At times we feel as though all of the hardships and difficulties we face are only for our demise, only to find out in the end that it really wasn't about us the at all, but that we were a chosen vessel handpicked by God to do work for His people.

For Such a Time as This

When an official of the King's Court named Haman plotted to have all of the Jews killed because of his hate for Esther's uncle Mordecai, Mordecai summoned the help of Esther. Because of her place in the kingdom, Mordecai knew that Esther could appeal to the king. Not knowing the meaning of her place or purpose in the kingdom, Esther refused her uncle's request.

Because of Esther's insecurities, she felt as though she didn't have the courage necessary to go before the king. This is one more thing that I love about God: He will never hold you accountable or responsible for those characteristics He has not given you. But if he has created an opportunity for assignment, no matter how hard we try to shirk from the responsibility, He expects us to deliver. When Esther's insecurities got the best of her, Mordecai ministered to her words that not only changed her life but also changed the course of a nation of people.

Mordecai advised Esther not to think that just because she was a part of the king's court that she would not be found out and her life would be spared as a Jew. He told her that if she remained silent in this time of distress of her people that God would raise up another deliverer, but her and her father's house would perish. He then prophesied to her past, present and future and said, "Yet who knows whether you have come to the kingdom for such a time as this?" In an instant Esther saw herself differently. She understood immediately the reason for her past. She understood the reason she'd been adopted, the reason she felt out of place and the reason she was chosen by God to be in the King's Court. For the first time, she felt in place. And in her right place, all feeling of insecurities was replaced with confidence and uncertainty with resolve. She replaced fear with faith and was ready to move forward in her purpose with God.

Our insecurities rob us of the necessary tools needed to accomplish God's plan for our life. When we identify and conquer our insecurities, we are able to live a life of courage and strength.

God desires for all of us, like Esther, to muster up enough faith and courage necessary to Awaken the Woman Within us. In doing so, we will not only cause blessings to flow within ourselves, but within those around us.

I pray that during our short journey together, you have made the decision to develop your authentic self and I hope that you are now committed to living the seven principles essential for developing your true self.

I began writing this book two years ago. My previous "start-stop" syndrome continued to get the best of me. What I learned since I began writing this book is that in order to be someone or something on the outside, you must first "be" on the inside. Despite my desire to write a great book to help women become their best selves, the heavens just wouldn't let me accomplish such a task without becoming my best self first. Although I have plenty of room to grow, I feel comfortable in declaring: I am better today than I was yesterday and as such, have been released to finish this book.

I have shared with you what the wisdom of the Holy Spirit has shared with me in my journey to excavate my authentic self in hopes that you too find peace with the woman within you.

I desire to hear from you. Please inform me of your progress on your journey or if you have found any of our principles to be of use to you. Email me your stories and I will share them with our online community at www.AzizahInc.com. Email me at info@AzizahInc.com and tell us what you are doing to ensure that you are a reflection of the woman God intended you to be, both inside and out.

Some journeys are more difficult than others, but the journey within is worth its weight in gold. I love you with the love of the Lord and pray that God will bless and prosper the work of your hands as He places with you the power to Awaken the Woman Within.

About the Author

Azizah Sulieman is a nationally recognized evangelist and public speaker.

As founder of The King's Daughter Summit and Fellowship, Azizah has become one the nations leading and prominent speakers of her generation. A noted author and life coach, she has impacted the lives of thousands of young women in the U.S. and abroad through her powerful and life changing messages. Azizah's passion is to assist women and girls in reaching their plight to discover their authentic purpose and destiny.

A native of Dayton, Ohio, Azizah knows first hand what it is to suffer from low self-esteem. Some of her life's most difficult challenges birthed the turning point of her path to self-discovery. Azizah knows the rewards of hard work, discipline and dedication.

Azizah is president of CommuniQuest, LLC a personal growth and consulting firm dedicated to the empowerment of corporate businesses and church administrators. She is a frequent speaker on college campuses across the country helping students to become equipped for their transition "From College to the Real World."

She has formed The Sulieman Corporation, a Community Development Corporation, which is in the beginning stages of forming Imani's House, a home for unwed teen mothers and The Center for Human Development.
As an Evangelist, her outreach ministry allows opportunities to share the gospel at women conferences, youth retreats and to congregations across the country. Within AzizahSpeaks Enterprises, she has delivered a series of messages, workshops and seminars based on the word of God that has changed the lives of many.

Azizah attended Wilberforce University where she earned a Bachelor of Arts degree in Mass Media Communications. Since leaving Wilberforce University, her journey as a speaker has brought her in front of many diverse audiences, crossing gender, racial and ethnic boundaries. She is the best selling author of, "Here to Stay! How I Made It Back as a Single Mother."

To Have AzizahSpeak at your next event
or to purchase other products contact:

AzizahSpeaks Enterprises

P.O. Box 92938
Washington, DC 20090
Executive Office 202-330-6313

Website: www.AzizahInc.com

Notes

CPSIA information can be obtained at www.ICGtesting.com
Printed in the USA
BVOW07s0231010714

357830BV00001B/3/A

9 780979 063008